And the Monster Swallows You Whole

Adrian S. Potter

STILL
HOUSE
PRESS

Copyright © 2023 Adrian S. Potter

First Edition

All Rights Reserved

No part of this book may be reproduced without written permission of the publisher.

All inquiries may be directed to:

> Stillhouse Press
> 4400 University Drive, 3E4
> Fairfax, VA 22030
> www.stillhousepress.org

Stillhouse Press is an independent, student and alumni-run nonprofit press based out of Northern Virginia and operated in collaboration with Watershed Lit: Center for Literary Engagement and Publishing Practice at George Mason University.

Library of Congress Control Number: 2023931138

ISBN-13: 978-1-945233-19-7

Cover Design: Megan Lynn Brooks
Cover Art: HayDmitriy via depositphotos
Interior Layout: Scott W. Berg

Thanks to the editors of the following journals and anthologies where versions of these pieces first appeared:

The Baltimore Review – "In Which Love is a Kind of Falling"
The Binnacle – "Simple Needs"
Brilliant Flash Fiction – "Marlboro Reds"
Claw & Blossom – "Rainy Season"
Colere – "Pop Quiz"
The Disappointed Housewife – "Angry Black Guy Looks: A Guide for New Employees"
Hairstreak Butterfly Review – "The Black Paragraphs"
Jet Fuel Review – "About These Poems"
The Journal of Compressed Creative Arts – "Sundown Town"
Lumiere Review – "Identity Theories"
The Maine Review – "Solving for X," "Room 213," "Can't Remember Like She Used to," "The Fall of Her Fall," "Never Home Anymore," "Partial Recall," "How Speech Therapy Can Become a Quest," "Mama Drama," "Mind Games" (published together under the title "The Half-Life of Human Memory")
Out of Line – "These Things Happen: The Understanding"
Panoplyzine – "Saturday Morning Remorse"
Paper Dragon – "Hope"
Pioneertown – "Notes for Novels I'll Never Write"
Pine Hills Review – "Entries From the Pandemic Diaries"
Poems of Political Protest: An Anthology – "A Black Guy Walks Into a Bar"
The Poet's Touchstone - "Why Sarah Left Her Husband"
Portage – "Lived Here Our Whole Lives," "Elegy for Rest Stop Towns"
Rat's Ass Review - "Freedom Isn't Free and Neither Are We"
Sonic Boom – "Glossolalia"
Talking Stick – "Storm Warning," "Suggestions for Writing Poetry," "These Things Happen," "The Difference Between Narrator and Author"
Wax Nine – "Token"

Contents

1 About These Poems

I Greetings from Flyover Country

5 Greetings from Flyover Country
6 Lived Here Our Whole Lives
7 Modern Desire
8 Rainy Season
9 Knee-High by the Fourth
10 Sundown Town
11 Life Cycle
12 Storm Warning
13 Origin Story
14 Marlboro Reds
15 Why Sarah Left Her Husband
16 In Which Love Is a Kind of Falling
17 Saturday Morning Remorse
18 Glossolalia
19 Winter Advisory
20 Joyride
21 Elegy for Rest Stop Towns

II The Half-Life of Human Memory

25 Solving for X
26 Room 213
27 The Fall of Her Fall
28 Can't Remember Like She Used To
29 Never Home Anymore
30 Partial Recall
31 Simple Needs
32 How Speech Therapy Can Become a Quest
33 Mama Drama
34 The Difference Between Narrator and Author
35 Mind Games

III The Black Paragraphs

39 Black Paragraph No. 1
40 These Things Happen: Holiday Shopping
41 Pop Quiz: Instructions and Question #1
42 Token
43 These Things Happen: Helping Hand
44 Black Paragraph No. 2
45 These Things Happen: Diversity
46 Black Paragraph No. 3
47 Freedom Isn't Free and Neither Are We
48 Pop Quiz: Question #2
49 These Things Happen: Some of My Best Friends
50 Black Paragraph No. 4
51 A Black Guy Walks Into a Bar and Says
56 These Things Happen: The Understanding
57 Pop Quiz: Question #3
58 Black Paragraph No. 5
59 These Things Happen: The Panhandler
60 Black Paragraph No. 6
61 Pop Quiz: Question #4
62 Angry Black Guy Looks: A Guide for New Employees
66 These Things Happen: Workiversary
67 Hope
68 Black Paragraph No. 7

IV Notes for Novels I'll Never Write

71 Working Title #1: "Full Moon Etude"
72 Working Title #2: "Apocalypse Survival Guide"
73 Working Title #3: "The Mourning Manual"
74 Working Title #4: "Haunted Moments"
75 Working Title #5: "Vanishing Act"
76 Working Title #6: "Confessions of a Dying Flame"

V Entries from the Pandemic Diaries

79 Sunday, February 23, 2020

80 Tuesday, February 25, 2020
81 Friday, March 13, 2020
82 Wednesday, March 25, 2020
83 Saturday, April 11, 2020
84 Tuesday, May 12, 2020
85 Thursday, May 21, 2020
86 Thursday, May 28, 2020
87 Saturday, June 6, 2020
88 Tuesday, June 16, 2020
89 Wednesday, July 1, 2020
90 Wednesday, July 15, 2020
91 Friday, August 7, 2020
92 Sunday, August 23, 2020
93 Tuesday, September 22, 2020

VI Identity Theories

97 1.
98 2.
99 3.
100 4.
101 5.
102 6.
103 7.
104 8.
105 9.
106 10.
107 11.
108 12.
109 13.
110 14.
111 15.
112 16.

115 Suggestions for Writing Poetry

About These Poems

These poems will not resurrect the past. These poems cannot make the sun move more quickly or slowly through the sky, cannot alter the inevitability of time. These poems won't erase a painful childhood or make maturity palatable. These poems refuse to clean messes, pay rent, keep secrets, or conjure magic. They will not find you a friend, not even if you recite them thrice before a mirror. They won't even be my friend and I authored the damned things. These poems cannot change luck, call for a cab, or drum up bail money. These poems do not pay attention. They are not vigilant listeners. They fail to keep quiet or give sound advice. You can only count on these poems to cheat at cards, drink the last beer from the fridge, and leave toilet seats up. These poems are not domesticated. All night you hear them brooding, craving freedom, cursing under their breath, begging to be released. Let them go.

I

Greetings from Flyover Country

Greetings from Flyover Country

In the middle of this nation, you'll find mystery. Township after township, each with a church and a tavern. Have a drink if you dare. Whiskey straight, no ice. Nice to see you. Nicer still to see you passing through these parts, wandering their hopelessly flat terrain. All the wrong turns past fields of sun-scorched soybeans are nothing but miles of rutted pavement laid over more rutted pavement. Roads proudly leading to unknown destinations. A flood of unhappy souls reeking of ditchwater and abandoned aspirations. Recently, a drifter shot himself dead in his pickup, his ghost now haunting the countryside with remorse. Your tug on the whiskey makes a sucking sound that echoes through the room, catches the attention of a brunette at the end of the bar. Buy her a drink. Stay for a while, your hands already shaking with desire.

Lived Here Our Whole Lives

Not happiness, not exactly. More like sunrise, or the routine of it, with haystacks and humidity perched on the horizon. Summer drying us out like neglected crops. In Iowa, the evenings feel disposable and star-crossed. The countryside flat as a supper plate. There is no language to translate the callouses on our hands, their deafening Braille. Bruises ripen on our bodies like plums. Nevertheless, we remain stoic, tight-lipped, subsisting on our diet of ritual and self-loathing. Gathering light in the folds of our work clothes. Singing our anthems, tipsy and fervent. We dream of lakeside campfires, evenings prone to the erratic weather of a spouse's temper. We remain restless as moths beating against porchlights, the ghosts of who we could've been haunting every trail between here and there.

Modern Desire

Temptation can be twisty with the truth. Constructed of loosened restraints and shifting morals, it sinks its teeth into the tender parts of our necks. Rides shotgun through bucolic landscapes littered with emptied beer cans and rotting trees. In the beginning, our impulses were content to hide inside backpacks and handbags, but now they crave freedom. Permission to argue with strangers on the internet, ride roughshod over the dreams of other desperate people, set virtual fires, and taunt the tenderhearted. In the liquor store, we keep finding new bottles to blame for our sketchy decisions. Our houses fill with wayward voices and moth-eaten curtains. Spring delivers dandelions to our doorsteps, caches of birds loitering on the power lines. They sing at night the way all mortal things do, as if their lives depend on it.

Rainy Season

After the flood, we can't remove the scent of the river from our boots. The drift of the current from our bones. Even in dreams, we drown like kidnapped girls that the police gave up searching for. Our clothes feel like gauze around our damp skin, our eyes become dull and ragged as gravel. Once we swam the width, bank to bank in a flash, slicing through the water around us. Even then it was growing within us, this need to escape. Our tainted faith, our forged futures, our botched deliverance. Now it pours outside for days, moisture swelling the door jambs, the tension aching like a rotten tooth. We grow accustomed to absence, the body's space, the void of existence. Already we pray for summer, hoping optimism will spread like wildflowers across the floodplain. We are losing ourselves, piece by piece, eroding like riverbanks, dirty water lapping at our ankles.

Knee-High by the Fourth

July scratches at the backdoor, breeds honeysuckle and contempt. Don't count your blessings until after the heatwave. Silence bores a hole within you, but hold fast. This season brings night sweats and fever dreams. Wolves gathering at the edge of the woods. The countryside consumes you bit by bit, but don't fight. Fall asleep, face-up, in the solace of a meadow. Be the landscape and the landscape will become you, dreary and endless. Be quiet, then quieter still. Each plot of earth watered by rivers other than your own. Tend to the crops, their growing promise. The piano wire that chokes out hope. Squeezing its throat, the ligature marking the way to our redemption.

Sundown Town

Everything begins to feel like a sacrifice. Finding vague threats at the property lines—wilted Black-eyed Susans, dead blackbirds, empty shotgun shells. The wind becomes a caveat, a sign. Caution lodged beneath weary tongues, haunting the intention of every explanation. On the kitchen table, we trace highways on a roadmap, outline each stop before departing. The out-of-the-way detours that unravel our patience one by one. Mind the stream that traces its way back to its origin. The identities we must lose to get there. The women that go missing every spring. The strangers following us to the city limits from the farmer's market. Their rage fills creek bottoms. Beware of truck stops, hanging trees, the ditches thick with fear and bluestem. *Don't be brown and around when the sun comes down.* Places where the moon pulls darkness over us like a tarpaulin until we escape or suffocate.

Life Cycle

Early July and the woods are buzzing with cicadas and secrets. Droning with shadows and predators lurking just beyond the perimeter of sight. At night, we lay down blankets and wait at the edge of a field. Wait for fireworks to punctuate the nocturnal sky as it attempts to swallow everything - the hillside, the driveway, the gate, the rusted pickup. Wait for everything we love to vanish and then reappear entirely changed. Summer shakes itself free inevitably, and inevitably, we lose our way back home. Back to the past, each dirt road leading us within spitting distance of liberation.

Storm Warning

Ask her for a story and the narrative unfurls like a spool of ribbon. How she clutched hope like a stuffed animal until harsh weather passed, huddled inside a storm shelter, body heat steaming over lanterns and dust-coated canning jars. Each summer, the winds came back around and blew through town like drifters ready to deliver chaos again. The somber wreckage of gas stations and lampposts hopelessly bent into vees, sycamores snapped like matchsticks. The lightning that flickered nervously through cracks in the cellar door. Her father perched on the top stair, hands wrapped tightly around the handle. Who'd have known she was open raw to the rainfall and squalls, the hatch of her mouth birthing things worse than catastrophe? Testimonials of how rebuilding can become so routine that you anticipate it, how pain sometimes lasts longer than the wound that invents it.

Origin Story

Yesterday the world tasted like dust rising from gravel roads. Even the wind chimes sparked paranoia and the ache of Bartlett pears decaying in the autumn sunlight. Maybe the sound of my name leaves you despondent, evokes a film where a lover waves goodbye from a bus station platform. Or confesses how the smokestacks and silos on the skyline desperately want to become a psalm. If you listen, you can hear the holes in my apologies, sounds illuminated by the tension in my muscles. Perhaps with this page, I could fashion false enthusiasm or a convincing excuse. A podunk town made entirely out of tiny disasters.

Marlboro Reds

Just past the fairgrounds, the girls abandon the road for the woods. Wander into a clearing, their jackets snagging on the low hanging branches of crabapple trees. The dappled light just enough to see flies gathering on the rotting fruit. Each girl's breath grows acrid from puffing on stolen cigarettes. One of them lifted a pack of smokes from their stepdad's nightstand, a moment molded by equal parts peer pressure and payback. Such luxuries must be enjoyed fast and with gusto. What they thought was adolescence, just another form of violence. What they thought was violence, just another autumn morning, crisp as a laundered bedsheet. Nobody anticipated danger as the secondhand smoke kissed the sky, as they tucked secrets under their tongues like breath mints.

Why Sarah Left Her Husband

Likely the vocabulary of silence, or the lies told on behalf of careless fists. Maybe the squabbles in front of the children, or artificial smiles tossed toward neighbors, or orphaned intentions that kept her static for too long. Probably the difficult explanations. A sheriff knocking on the door. Or patience, worn thin as rice paper. Certainly the ache of her ribs, or the bruises lining her wrists, empurpled as the evening sky. Definitely what we call interruption, the illusion of closure, the insults grudgingly swallowed like bitter medicine. Surely the blade-sharpened seconds between fury and fear, or apprehension measured by the number of anniversaries celebrated. Perhaps the damaged mementos, misguided devotion, or infinity inside her mouth, burning.

In Which Love Is a Kind of Falling

Rumors shake up the town like a bag of marbles. Shift them enough and they fall out the mouth, smooth and black as tar. A proliferation of lies makes me jittery, which is to say, there are far worse things than the truth. Me, I've been writing letters to the Midwestern sky and mailing them to the wrong addresses. Darling, I'm so dry these days that I could turn to dust, but I have big plans, multifaceted but subject to coding errors. A kind of cryptography, prone to hidden meanings and hysteria. You do this thing where you leave me, but it's a confidence game, sleight of hand, something I trick into happening. You always come back, eventually, like a hotel pool you've been crashing for years. Like an eclipse, or dark spot in my vision. You shine so bright it's intoxicating, which is to say, it's terrifying.

Saturday Morning Remorse

By sunrise, there's a whole plotline written in my breath. A tinge of schnapps, of tobacco. An allegory sleeping in the nude beside me, convenient amnesia cloaking portions of the narrative. I'm neither less nor more innocent than anyone else, scribbling my name with a finger on a mirror, shower steam condensation becoming a backdrop for my signature. Truth is, we've all fallen for it. Nights muddled in moonshine and the silent unfastening of buttons. Another cautionary tale. A twisted path where I stumble, misled by curvature. By checkout time, I evacuate the room to stop my conscience from reeling. Burn the clothing to kill the stench. Something about the vagueness in my voice disquiets me. Anxiety has a house and a fence and a loaded shotgun on the front porch. A Molotov cocktail. A lit match.

Glossolalia

Autumn still aches in her joints. Filters through her flesh like the scent of spoiled leftovers. She's a miscast spell, an exit wound, a blind curve. Near the jukebox, she leans too close to strangers who are highly suspect, lip-syncs tequila's clichéd hymn. Sometimes the night sharpens itself against her edges. Evokes a restlessness that rises beneath her ribs like bread. The flowers on her dress, tiny blooms culled in a field of pale blue, could trigger a revelation, a reluctant sermon of desire hiding inside her mouth. She's trying to locate salvation amid the sheets by feel, by guessing. The mattress swollen with hallelujahs and regrets.

Winter Advisory

Whatever you do, don't let pessimism sink its hooks into you. It might seem alluring from a distance, but up close, the monster swallows you whole. Too many stiff drinks and karaoke nights laying the groundwork for dubious decisions. Soon, every lake is frozen over, the fish swimming the depths for survival. Reach deep into snowdrifts, deep towards the waning sun. Deep inside the house where field mice nest in the walls. How they know nothing of winter's fangs gnawing the gentle landscape. Know nothing of death, the lure and sudden snap of life's carefully laid traps.

Joyride

Along Route 5, a pickup crosses the double yellow line while taunting fate and quashing premonitions. Streaks through forgettable townships with names like Anna and Stacy. Recognizes things happen until they don't. Inventory the inconsistencies in my backstory and you'd know I am a liar, my quivering tongue split like a tuning fork. Each swindle is an utterance that begins in the diaphragm and pickpockets our common sense. The headlights cast doubt onto the asphalt, skim the shadows of cattails. Still, I fear stopping. The word *destination* becomes muffled and uncertain. A place where the world gets broken in like work boots. Where logic plays hide-and-seek within the radio's static hum.

Elegy for Rest Stop Towns

Heading west on I-80, you learn the art of loneliness. Begin to think of travel as spaces opening to more spaces, each one more vast than the last. Past the Missouri River, the cities get smaller and smaller until they're just blips along the journey. Something you might mistake for a myth if you didn't know better. If you hadn't lived in one of those locations for years with barely a breath or a sigh. A slight cough. Often enough, drivers came through seeking gas or directions. All that space to wander, but you stayed there listening to semis roll past. As, little by little, the world crumbled around you. The spaces inside you are far more open than the fields spreading themselves against the skyline. That yawn and gape into the prairie horizon.

II

The Half-Life of Human Memory

Solving for X

Some health problems attack methodically—cancer, heart disease, the slow siphoning of the body's vigor as it ages. But more worrisome are the unpredictable things that happen without warning, when hard luck and outside forces co-author tales of tragedy.

There's a reason I frequently walk the same route home. A reason why I routinely eat the same lunch at work, carefully counting calories and carbohydrates. If I learned anything from all that math in school, it's easier to solve for X if you limit the number of other variables.

No surprises allowed. Ever. I never want to mutter *I don't know why X happened*. So I keep the algorithms of my days coded tight and consistent.

My mother often chooses to improvise. Instead of patiently waiting for me or my brothers to visit, she climbed onto a step stool to change a light bulb that was just out of reach. After a clumsy fall, a cognitive fog settled in her brain, with no sign of lifting.

She gets better, then worse. X happened. I don't know why. Now I'm stuck trying to find answers to my mom's cold equations.

Room 213

This hospital has become a familiar destination that we return to reluctantly. The walls are painted a soothing shade of sage, but everything else feels numbly uncomfortable. My mother is more often asleep than she is awake. The medical machines continue beeping their desperate cadence, blending with the sterile drone of a television that's on only to fill the awkward silence. The uncertain trajectory of recovery stumbles like a drunk down a dark hallway.

The Fall of Her Fall

It's October, so all the critters outside instinctively seek warmth once it vanishes. Start their annual home invasions, seeking asylum, trying to become autumnal refugees. Notice how falling temps can make feral things yearn for a domestic existence. Mice hide behind appliances while boxelder bugs congregate in cellars. Pulling into the driveway after dark, I spot a raccoon loitering by the garage, wondering why all the trash cans remain empty. Squirrels leave paw print graffiti in the frost on the deck, linger in the yard at sunrise, and nip off the ends of oak branches. Lately, the animals seem bolder. Mom's never home.

Can't Remember Like She Used To

After the accident, my mom stops noticing things, aside from an occasional insect creeping along the floorboards. Or a wayward moth flitting against a smudged windowpane. Confusion enters her mind deliberately like syrup through an IV. I visit every few days for an overnight. She always recognizes me, but as somebody else—one of my brothers, or the ghost of my father, or some former co-worker whose name pops up in her mental scrapbook before mine. A spider in the corner promises to stay on his side of the room while sadness collects like dust on the sheer curtains.

Never Home Anymore

Without notice, the landlord cuts down two maple trees outside my window. Suddenly there are gangs of displaced birds I've never noticed before, panhandling for crumbs on the sidewalk. The insects that feasted on our blood all summer slowly disappear as autumn rises. Now only bite occasionally during unseasonably warm days. My dogs succumb to savage impulses whenever I leave them alone too long, shitting in the hallway and gnawing on the shoes by the front door. Nothing but silence and pet dander floating through an empty apartment, rent money paid on time just for furniture to amass more dust.

Partial Recall

In rehab, the therapist asks Mom to name the animals on the flashcards—*dog, horse, cow.*

Each identification takes more effort than the previous one. Her attention oscillates, exhibits the half-life of human memory. Laughing, she reminisces about a Holstein her parents had on the farm of her childhood, then gazes at the linoleum, paralyzed by muddled reasoning. Answers gestate awkwardly in her mind, arthritic hands forcing plastic triangles into star-shaped holes. *What is your name? What city are we in? What day is your birthday?*

She rolls her eyes, impatient with the lady who cheerfully interrogates her—*cat, pig, mouse.*

Simple Needs

Hoping to hotwire her memory, I compile a collage for my mom's birthday, a patchwork of photos spanning generations. In one picture, I'm no older than three, wearing some awful T-shirt, my Afro uncombed and desperately needing a trim. Mom towers above me, the corners of her mouth bowing upward into a familiar smile. My fingers stretch toward heaven, intercepted by her cocoa-butter-softened palm.

We're standing by the tree that guards the entrance to my parents' driveway. During my lifetime, several vehicles will donate paint to its trunk in failed attempts to back out. I'll even dent my Ford Escort on it, one week after buying it used with money saved from a summer job.

But at the time of the photograph, I didn't have a job, a car, or any idea of how a tree could be an unavoidable obstacle. All I had was the assurance of my mother's hand, and that was all I needed.

How Speech Therapy Can Become a Quest

Over the next few visits, she relearns new animals. Rediscovers facts she already knew like unearthing jars of money that she forgot were buried in her garden.

Each week, panic skulks like an untamed beast outside the clinic and refuses to leave. Words scratch her throat like fishbones and choke her mid-response. *Elephant, tiger, alligator*.

Mom's tentative cadence mimics the sluggish pace of recovery. There's a mythical creature inside me that must be slain, along with the reflexive anxiety I feel whenever a phone rings unexpectedly.

Can you say one more on your own?
She pauses, then utters *dragon*.

Mama Drama

In fiction, mothers often get taken for granted. Literature, like the blues, is a refuge for those with tattered souls, uneasy hearts, and woeful sighs. Weary-eyed with ragged patience, they wander through hallways chained by regrets. Reluctantly wallow in minor losses. Clutch onto them like flashlights during a blackout. Collect toxic relationships and familial sacrifices like Girl Scout merit badges, then wear them with silent pride. The truth is, I've figuratively killed more literary mothers than I've revived, perpetually grieving over their corpses. They start to litter attics and crawlspaces. Chubby and slender. Hungover and hopeless. Youthful and senile.

The Difference Between Narrator and Author

I hesitantly hand my mother a copy of my first book with a disclaimer. *Where it says I, that's not always me.*

Later Mom cross-examines me about my replicas, each one Frankensteined together from crude metaphors and poetic license. She gets hung up on every sonnet's mythology like a bedsheet on a clothesline. My clones walk past and ignore my mother, untethered to identity. I wish I could claim I mourned each one with their leather jackets and dubious attitudes, but they start to pile up in the poems like garbage. So heavy that I can't lug them more than a few feet without pausing. Until I finally douse them with gasoline and light them ablaze.

Where it says I, that's not always me.

I gently echo this explanation of a literary device, feeling guilty for secretly wishing I could become one of my poetic duplicates, no longer duty-bound to repeat myself to a mother who sometimes hears but never fully understands.

Mind Games

Mom would sit at the kitchen table, her morning coffee adjacent to a newspaper folded awkwardly to the page with the brainteasers. Handwriting indecipherable as cuneiform, crosswords graffitied with scribbles, sloppy proof of her daily ritual to remain sharp. *You gotta use it or lose it.* Solve each 11 down, every 32 across. How I helped with the clues that stumped her, the ones about computers or pop culture. How my memory also seems sketchy since I can't recall precisely when Mom stopped working those puzzles. How everyone's identity degrades, eventually, leaving only what we haven't forgotten about ourselves, yet.

III

The Black Paragraphs

Black Paragraph No. 1

Sometimes, we die of such blackness, after becoming a smudge on the margins. Slice right through layers of scar tissue with a boning knife. We are all about wanting, waiting, and weariness. Something as American as insider trading or institutional prejudice. If we kill it, we can name it. This open wound bleeding on the fringes, this tension, this contrast between shades. How we kick the can down the road instead of tossing it in the trash. We loiter on street corners in American neighborhoods knowing our presence has American implications that linger in the minds of some who protect and serve. Their disdain seems familiar and sinister and still undoubtedly American. We wait with held breath for change. We see it directly in front of us, yet it remains as elusive as it is desirable. We wait for our ache to subside, for the slow-burning hallelujah of healing to arrive.

These Things Happen: Holiday Shopping

It's Christmas time. You and your mother battle through, a crowded department store. Unsupervised kids flood the toy section. Some misbehave yanking action figures from their packaging, pointing water guns and plastic swords at each other, shrieking and sprinting through aisles as if they were at an indoor playground.

You see a neon mini-basketball. Without thinking, you snatch it off the shelf and dribble twice on the linoleum, which registers as a blip on the commotion scale compared to the hubbub of the other children.

Mom scowls and pulls you aside. You hear the subtle venom in her voice as she hisses, "Boy—don't do things that will get you noticed. People are already watching you. You're black."

Pop Quiz: Instructions and Question #1

Instructions

> You have twenty minutes to complete this quiz. Answer all four questions thoroughly, based on the facts and ideas that you have learned through life experience. You will be graded on the honesty, logic, and cultural sensitivity shown in your responses. All work must be your own; any usage of classmates, notes, smartphones, or textbooks is strictly prohibited. You may begin work now.

Question #1

> Two applicants are vying for the same position at a prestigious advertising agency. Both candidates are African-American males with comparable educational backgrounds, experience, and computer skills. Both seem articulate and personable, so they would fit in well with the corporate culture of the company. Both guys also claim to be seeking long-term employment. One man is named Bradley Newton, while the other is named LaTavian Woods.

Q: Based only on the information given, which man receives the job offer? Discuss the pros and cons of this choice.

For extra credit, calculate the difference in lifetime earnings between these two men, considering projected time spent unemployed, base salary, 401k earnings, and annual bonuses. Show your work.

Token

Truth is, people will pretend
to like you if you simply stay
quiet. If you smile for no reason.

Each day, you drop stereotypes
like tarnished coins down wishing wells.
Dress up preconceived notions in a suit
and attend meetings. Nod and agree
with supervisors who know nothing
but a diluted version of you, yet
they keep banging up against the sharp edges
of your identity and bleeding all over the office.

How they never believe
you're like them until they realize
you aren't. How they say you sound nicer
on the phone. Or seem nicer in emails.
Nicer if you'd open your mouth
and allow *yes* to fly out abruptly
like a flock of spooked seagulls.

These Things Happen: Helping Hand

After a meeting, a co-worker laments over his struggles to repair his home computer. Since you're a bit of a tech geek, you kindly offer to stop over after work and help.

To your surprise, you are told that you would not be welcome in his house. He says, as a matter of fact, you would not be welcome in his neighborhood because of the old mindset that exists there.

From then on, you keep your distance in the office. But weeks later you overhear him, again bellyaching about the same computer issue. You laugh to yourself. Old mindsets evidently can't fix modern problems.

Black Paragraph No. 2

We've become your very favorite scapegoat, your favorite spectacle. Complete with trap doors in our bodies that open to secret rooms full of neglected dreams. Strange notions push us to fret over backhanded praises and question synthetic outrage. Such vastness is terrifying, the unmapped void of our collective identity. Darkness spreads its tentacles across the infrastructure of our souls, shrieks like a scalding-hot teakettle. The melancholia of our displaced smiles takes up a lot of attention, but we still recite mantras and spirituals by memory, sugar our voices into defiant whispers. Gust and swarm until nothing remains but typecasts and perceptions that loiter on the wrong side of town. You see us underneath the flickering bulbs of streetlamps. Our reluctant halos of illumination.

These Things Happen: Diversity

The media has made it trendy, but *diversity* is slowly becoming a hollow word. A void. People ask you to fill that void. Eventually, you become the void. This is called being accepted. You're supposed to like it. Breathe easy. Exhale.

Black Paragraph No. 3

From this vantage point, all our people are in danger. All our people buried alive by armfuls of abuse and superficial apologies. I do not know what to say when our nerves split and twinge. The inevitable movement of our hands to our mouths cupped with surprise. Only that I speak in strained metaphors about racism straining society. Only that the slick tongues of reporters continue spinning their convenient narratives inside echo chambers. Only that I laugh, but only because I could die laughing here, with tattered patience and sanity slow-leaking like a pinpricked tire. From this vantage point, we could turn our faces away from the system, but something oppressive hovers over us. It keeps pressing a pillow hard into our faces, suffocating us into silence, into submission.

Freedom Isn't Free and Neither Are We

We are lifelong investors in the dying business
of survival. We know where all the landmines are
and how long before they'll detonate. Racism
isn't hypothetical to us. We're expected to ignore
insults, systematic struggles, the slow smolder
of anger under our skin. We swallow society's
hatred like sour medicine. Side effects include
unwarranted bullets, nightstick contusions, loss
of breath due to chokeholds, ligature marks from
handcuffs. Social media erects a virtual platform
where people lob threats at a man who kneels quietly
during an anthem that was penned by a slave owner.
New tragedies weekly, innocents shot and falling
so fast even gravity has to be surprised. Hope is left
behind to drown in the pool of grief puddling
underneath bodies on the pavement. Each news
story teaches us liberty is a variable in an intricate set
of equations. Hoodie equals suspect. Minority equals
guilty. Fits the description equals black. Protesters
equal rioters. Nothing in the streets or on the internet
is safe. Everything is hazardous, even this poem.
We covet independence without danger. We want
to reclaim our destinies without cost. We get distracted
for no good reason. Overlooked and underpaid,
too wrapped up in our salaried gigs and side hustles
to recognize the static movement of change.
There is a source code for survival based on race,
religion, class, gender, and sexual preference.
Tolerance is an idealistic tangle of knots casually
tossed in the garbage. Like a bitter neighbor,
society knocks and asks me to turn down the volume
of my outrage. But instead, I scream. Louder.

Pop Quiz: Question #2

Question #2

> A white man has spent twenty-two years living in a government-subsidized housing project. His roots are on the north side of a major metropolitan area, in a less-affluent neighborhood where he is actually the minority. This man has grown up immersed in hip-hop culture and he closely follows the latest urban fashion trends. He almost exclusively listens to rap music.
>
> Nearly all of his friends are African-American. He was the only white person on the basketball team during his senior year. The man has been seriously dating his high school sweetheart, who is African-American, for five years. He plans on proposing to her next month.

(a) Considering his background and cultural influences, has this man ever said "the n-word" or an equivalent racial slur during his lifetime?

(b) If the answer to (a) is no, does he have a right to use such words based on where he has grown up and his close associations with African-Americans?

(c) If the answer to (a) is yes, how many times has he said it? Round your answer to a multiple of five.

These Things Happen: Some of My Best Friends

"But some of my best friends are black," he says with a pretentious smirk, as if this unproven statement exonerates him from any damage caused by his reckless remarks. Or as if people who claim to be open-minded maintain an inventory of friendships categorized by race, religious background, sexual preference, etc.

You look at your hands, already squeezed into eager fists, your mind entertaining the dare of punching his face – if only to test his hypothesis, to verify whether any of the buddies who would rescue him from an ass-whipping are indeed black.

The first punch lands squarely on his jaw.

Black Paragraph No. 4

The angels chant all night, crooning hymns for the fallen innocents that we immortalize as hashtags or on T-shirts. I can't tolerate the status quo. I can't tolerate anything but the long, gradual roll towards equality. But then again, none of us are getting out of this alive or intact. The children cursed to have scratch-and-dent spirits. Their parents rummaging for remnants of hope on dollar store shelves. Everyone else pretending things will get better and going on and on about progress. Even politicians know the jig is up, with the veneer of democracy on fire and this deliberate creep towards dystopia. Regret touches everything prejudice touches, but then again, prejudice touches everything—sutured communities, candlelight vigils, peaceful marches, feral uprisings. The world inhales as heaven catches hell above us.

A Black Guy Walks into a Bar and Says

Let's start with chattel slavery because
why wouldn't we? The one where people
were chained into forced migration

for free labor—no, it was not a virtual reality
RPG with subpar graphics and a cringeworthy
story arc. And let's consider how there is

a hint of invisibility within our identities.
How our voices break silence like bullwhips
cracking against skin. And let's not disregard

the verbal abuse. Who takes responsibility
for this, anyway? It's an American thing
to scream hateful things in public or

on Twitter and then blame the victims
for what was said. If not, it seems like it.
Think of implied threats and dog-whistle

politics. Unidentified rage against those
who fit the description. I asked peers what
they thought of this and they mentioned

sit-ins, sideways glances, stop-and-frisk, and
survival strategies. Excuse me, but I've hinted
at a stereotypical plotline we've all witnessed

before. Honestly, I also worry about oil
pipelines running through the Dakotas.
About government evil-scheming behind

executive orders. Politicians are planting
seeds of hatred in our backyards but it'll
be okay—this is due process, so sit back

and watch those weeds grow. I apologize
if nothing bothers you, but I have been
bothered my entire life. This brings me

back to the echoes of slave songs, hymns
of the repressed and stressed. Does it seem
like overkill? Only if the same people

get killed, over and over. That's a hot take,
but what isn't these days? When somebody
crafted the social construct of race, the side

effects were intentional. When people pilfered
Native lands, they relabeled theft as *manifest
destiny*. When they heard about our pain,

they blamed their ancestors but said we need
to get over it. I am over it, maybe. Maybe not.
Maybe what I'm saying is that human history

hasn't always been orchestrated humanely.
We are breathing byproducts of implicit bias.
Conformity is the dullest version of reality,

but the one most familiar to us. Sometimes
I speak in another voice for acceptance. Maybe
it's yours. I won't apologize. I won't apologize for

apologizing when probably I shouldn't have.
Between 1932 and 1972, groups of African-
American men unwittingly became experiments

for the government. How the Public Health
Service deceived them for scientific purposes.
How syphilis studies trumped ethics. How we

can't hear a coronavirus vaccine mentioned
without the ghosts of Tuskegee haunting
our thoughts. Meanwhile, the puppets don't

want to admit they are puppets, so all our strings
keep getting manipulated. Yet we deftly built
a culture out of counterculture and christened it

hip hop. Now we rap, DJ, and graffiti every
building and wave our hands in the air until
the break of dawn. A breakdancing motion.

Popping and locking with soulful contortions
of body and spirit. We watch as hope misses
its intended target like an errant military drone.

Yet we remix the wrongs and make a mixtape
of this nation's mistakes. We put it out on
streaming services and let your brother nod

his head to it, let your mama sing along off-key
and botch the lyrics. Our dreams are the origin
of a storybook ending that was edited out of

the script. Think about craving equality and
liberty from a country that doesn't want us
to have them. We can't claim to be African

just as we really can't claim to be American.
History carved a canyon-like space between
identities with a hyphenated tightrope for us

to traverse. It's not just tiptoeing across that's
treacherous, but also the hazard of not knowing
what's on the other side. A familiar uncertainty

that can birth multiple headaches or a miscarriage
of justice. Language is accustomed to being colonized
by subtle deception in the name of what's allegedly

right, so I'd rather not take this fight to your neck.
It might stifle creativity or limit productive dialogue.
Instead, keep running until you reach the edge of

your identity. And jump off. And savor the dulcet
seconds between falling and crashing. You must
wake up before you can stay woke. Weeks after

the election, we feel uneasy in the presence of each
other. A wolfish feeling scratches at the door, skulks
through neighborhoods after midnight. Each morning

becomes a fistful of life swinging towards our faces.
Reality hits us over the head like an empty Budweiser
bottle in a barfight. I'd claim we will survive, but we're

clueless, crowdfunding our downfall without realizing
it, lynching ourselves subconsciously with the nooses
inside our minds. It's as American as income inequity

and arrogance. The record of the human condition gets
warped with age. Since love is a drowning thing,
we turned our hearts into oceans. Change happens,

inevitably, when somebody resists it, like suffrage
and desegregation. How all this pours out from
my fingers like cheap liquor on sidewalks for those

who rest in power. Pours out like unfiltered opinions
from TV reporters, even if we more often use social
media as a news source, anyways. We interrupt your

regularly scheduled programming to bring you this
announcement: the margins don't hide themselves
well. And they don't hide us, either. At schools, why

do we appear so uncomfortable? At foodie restaurants,
why do we look so irritated? It's rude to ask for freedom
to be served without a side order of backlash, so we've

been told. Perhaps the fresh injustice would be a better
choice. Locally sourced, says the menu in Garamond font.
Some people would rather drink some hazy IPAs at home

and binge-watch the revolution on Hulu. Alexa, please
set a reminder: feign outrage online next Tuesday.
Don't smile and touch our hair to confirm it feels

different than yours. Don't lightheartedly compare
your post-vacation tan to our melanin. Don't think
buying us a Crown & Coke at happy hour will erase

our memory of the insensitive joke you told before
an office meeting. Our existence is not a punchline.
A black guy walks into a bar and says a whole lot

of heavy-duty, thought-provoking shit, but people
just laugh since *he's always so funny* and *he speaks
so well* and *he isn't like all those other black guys*

who frequently trigger them into feeling excessively
awkward or annoyed or anxious. Sigh. I could keep
going but this joke must end. This joke must end.

These Things Happen: The Understanding

It seems harmless at first. They are a cluster of corporate clones, seven mid-life crisis victims enjoying happy hour. It looks like a light beer commercial. They are fully engaged in cheerful chitchat; you assume it is about fatherhood or fantasy football.

You proceed over to their table, but only because it's your job. You jot down their order, some expensive microbrews with orange wedges. The talking and snickering resume once you leave. You wonder what's so hilarious but remain focused on your work.

The problem with being a good listener is you often pay attention to things you aren't intended to hear. While you're tending to a mess at a nearby table, one of the men clearly says, "Two niggers walk into a bar..."

Racial jokes. Your ethnicity is a punch line in their personal stand-up comedy special. You glare at the businessmen, your body wrapped in a cocoon of shock. And they continue laughing, laughing like their ancestors probably did when they whipped your ancestors, laughing like they'd consider shackling your black ass if that pesky 13th Amendment hadn't been ratified.

One guy eventually senses your anger and apologizes with the transparent sincerity of a politician. The others quiet down while you shake his hand with all the professionalism you can muster. You bitterly retreat to the bar and pour their drinks. You contemplate giving your manager two weeks' notice, but you really need to keep this gig.

While you wiggle each mug slightly so that your nigger saliva will mix perfectly with their craft beers, a childhood memory comes to mind. Your dad once said, "Never work at a place where you have to take other people's bullshit with a smile."

At this moment, you understand exactly what your father meant.

Pop Quiz: Question #3

Question #3

> A veteran security guard at an upscale department store receives an urgent call on his two-way radio saying there's a shoplifter on the first floor. He quickly abandons his fourth-floor post to stop the thief from leaving the premises with merchandise. As he runs downstairs, the reception on his walkie-talkie fades, so he cannot hear the full description of the shoplifter.
>
> As he bursts onto the first floor, he spots four different customers heading off towards four different exits.
>
> One is an elderly Asian lady, who has an oversized purse that could hold a lot of stolen goods.
>
> The second is a destitute-looking, African-American woman wearing a bulky winter coat that has a surplus of pockets.
>
> Heading towards the third door is a Caucasian man dressed in a three-piece pinstriped suit; he is suspiciously clutching a briefcase that is half-open.
>
> The fourth suspect is a heavily-pierced Latinx teenager sporting several tattoos and a baseball cap.

Which person does the security guard chase down? Does his choice make him a bad person? Prove your work.

Black Paragraph No. 5

A few more moments and we might disappear into the background. Vanish into the ether of expectations. Our culture dissolving into the mist, our unnatural selection into gentrification. No sooner do we place ourselves against the system and gaze toward the future than the past starts torturing our spirits. Our spines sore from shouldering residual shame and artificial bravado. But then who knows which inheritance weighs more? Who knows which way the storyline will be spun, exploited, and exported? The blues sound bluer here, more downhearted than expected. Our thoughts are fleeting and fragmented. A few more moments and the threats all change, our cheeks exposed to society's backhand as it pimps us into oblivion.

These Things Happen: The Panhandler

A man outside of the parking ramp is asking for handouts. Normally you're at least good for the loose change in your pocket, but he's wearing a t-shirt embossed with a Confederate flag. So you walk past, wordlessly.

Black Paragraph No. 6

Folks can't handle our anger, translate our vernacular, or relate to our attitude. They cover us with blanket statements, claim we require coaching and counseling, yet only prod and provoke. So we stay opinionated, defiant, but always camera-ready. When you gossip about us in office breakrooms or school hallways, we hear it. We've been taking punches since kindergarten, so fighting is in our muscle memory. Temper, temper. Never mind the smudged napkin sketches we've crafted to approximate our identities. Or the whip's bite against the skin of our forebearers. We've relayed familiar pleas about adverse conditions to dead ears for centuries. So stop with all the *now more than ever* hyperbole. The distance separating *now* and *ever* endlessly approaches nil, until it becomes *now more than ever, forever ever, forever ever*.

Pop Quiz: Question #4

Question #4

> Two African-American males, Al and James, started working at the same firm seven years ago. Both are ambitious college graduates who use their intelligence and charisma to the fullest. They have advanced in their professional development, and both are due for upper-level promotions. These two guys are the only employees of their ethnicity in the company. Al and James consider each other good friends, and they are also respected by clients and peers.
>
> Both men are African-American, but skin color is where the similarities in their appearance end. Al dresses business casual, keeps his hair in a low-cropped, wavy style, and has a full-grown beard. James has a completely shaven head, typically has a thin mustache, and dresses fancily, often wearing designer ties and sport coats. These two guys look nothing alike, yet their co-workers sometimes say "Hello Al" when greeting James in the hallway, and vice versa. This mistake happens periodically, but always seemingly by accident.

Q: Is one of these workers justified in feeling offended when he's inadvertently called by the other's name? Should this type of mistaken identity still be taking place after this many years of loyal employment? Why or why not?

Angry Black Guy Looks: A Guide for New Employees

As a longtime employee of XYZ Corporation, I'd like to welcome you to the company!

I am genuinely excited to have you on the team. Undoubtedly, you'll discover some coworkers refer to me as the "Angry Black Guy" of this firm, likely due to the irritated looks I give during meetings, office get-togethers, and routine communication. But I assure you these looks don't just represent anger; each one corresponds to a reaction triggered by a specific scenario.

I'd like to start on the right foot as colleagues, so I've assembled a summary of what these looks actually mean. Please review and ask questions as needed to ensure our interactions remain transparent, honest, and cordial. Refer to this list often and I believe you'll become well versed with all of these–and recognize they shouldn't be simply categorized as anger.

- Please Don't Feel Obligated to Say Hello Look
- I'm Not Exactly Sure This Is a Good Morning Look
- You Just Said Something Overtly Racist and Don't Even Realize It Look
- Thank You So Much for Stealing My Idea in Front of Our Boss Look
- Oh, So You Want to Talk About the Weather When I Have a Deadline Look
- You Have Absolutely Nothing to Contribute to This Meeting Look

- ☐ Just Because You Said It Louder Doesn't Mean You're Correct Look
- ☐ I Had Headphones on So I Didn't Hear Anything You Said Look
- ☐ I Am Politely Holding in Urges to Cuss at You Look
- ☐ If You Had Any Ethics Then You Wouldn't Need to Ask that Question Look
- ☐ Stop Repeating What I Already Said Look
- ☐ Stop Repeating What You Already Said Look
- ☐ Don't Compare Your Tan to My Natural Pigmentation Look
- ☐ I'm Not Convinced that Neon Funky Print Skinny Tie Makes You Cool Look
- ☐ This Probably Won't Achieve What You Hope It's Going to Achieve Look
- ☐ Do You Talk Down to Others Because You Can't Get It Up Look
- ☐ Stop Smiling While Delivering Shitty News Look
- ☐ I'm Trying to Cope with You Completely Wasting My Time Look
- ☐ You're Going to Ignore the Mess You Made in the Lunchroom Look

- [ ] I'm Waiting For You to Ask for My Opinion Look

- [ ] No, That's the Name of the Other Black Dude In Our Department Look

- [ ] I'm Deciding Whether I Care About All This Look

- [ ] If I'm Reading Too Much Into Something, It's More Reading Than You've Ever Done Look

- [ ] The Facts You Just Shared with Me Are Blatant Lies Look

- [ ] I Suspect You Are Overly Sensitive to Any Form of Feedback Look

- [ ] Your Outrage Is Slightly Humorous to Me Look

- [ ] I'm Not Throwing That Pity Party You Want Look

- [ ] You're Going to Get Me Called into HR Look

- [ ] How Can This Presentation Be So Long Yet Say Nothing Look

- [ ] I'm Surviving This Social Situation by Comparing It to That Time I Got Hazed Look

- [ ] I Resent Having to Take You Seriously Look

- [ ] If You Tell Jokes About Other Races Then I'm Pretty Sure You Say The N-Word Look

- [ ] Interrupt Me Again and I'll Body Slam You Against the Copier Look

- [ ] I Would Strongly Suggest You Cease Speaking Look

- [ ] Stop Repeating Commonly Known Motivational Quotes as if You Made Them Up Look

- [ ] Thank You for Continuing to Blather as You Follow Me into a Public Restroom Look

- [ ] Your Level of Smugness Would Be Amazing if It Wasn't Repugnant Look

- [ ] Don't Feel Obligated to Like Me Look

- [ ] I No Longer Feel Obligated to Like You Look

- [ ] Your Defensiveness Is Sometimes Entertaining Look

- [ ] This Might Be a Good Day to Leave Early Look

- [ ] Don't Stop by Just to Gossip When I'm Trying to Get Out of Here Look

These Things Happen: Workiversary

There's one other black guy in your company, Greg, and by chance you both start at the firm on the same day. Soon you grow tired of correcting people, so sometimes you answer to the wrong name. You get accustomed to saying "no worries" when you're mistaken for another man who you look nothing like. Maybe you even flash a smile, only to make the older, white managers feel more comfortable about their blunder. "It's no big deal." How could they be expected to see you both as individuals? To see the differences between their two quota fillers, the twin tokens, the dual diversity statistics?

You're an optimist and overachiever, so you assume the confusion will eventually wane. At some point during your career, people will figure out who is who. An awesome performance or terrible blunder will distinguish one of you from the other. Time passes and the mix-ups happen less frequently.

During an office event, supervisors hand out plaques and accolades to employees who have been working there for ten years. A decade at a job is a big deal, and you're humbly proud of this achievement. You and several others stand in front of the remaining staff and receive awards and polite applause. You are silently relieved that no one prods you into giving an awkward impromptu speech. Towards the end of the festivities, you look down and realize the name on the plaque that you're holding is not yours.

You and Greg swap plaques afterwards, away from everybody else. You both laugh it off, but neither of you finds it funny. Greg conjures up a feeble excuse for the mistake and then says flatly, "These things happen."

And yes, it's true, these things do happen. But they really shouldn't.

Hope

You are trapped inside a poem
that's part dungeon, part safe space,
a storm shelter surrounded by squalls.
You are part mailman, part machete,
delivering handwritten notes of optimism
to the severed hands of unlucky recipients.

You are not the food on the table
but the urge that drags us there,
starving. I label you as both savior
and scapegoat in the same breath.
You preach sermons about the rope
without mentioning the tree,
neglecting the asphyxiated truth
hanging between us.

I imagine you as a specter of light
with a lump of burning coal for a heart.
Voltas of gentrified dreams,
brutal futures, and melancholy equations.

You survive only because some people
want you to exist. You survive only because
other people want you destroyed.

Black Paragraph No. 7

Best believe we've mapped out an escape plan for when things inevitably come undone. Fuck with us and it will get so real. We didn't make it this far just to befriend enemies. Every second we breathe, we're expected to forgive. Governments spit their shade, so we spit back, middle fingers raised. We're free, but under onerous terms and conditions. Our foreheads loiter in the clouds, toes rooted in hallowed terrain. We remain groundbreaking. Brooding, belligerent, brave, branded by the struggle. Otherwise, black.

IV

Notes for Novels I'll Never Write

Working Title #1: "Full Moon Etude"

<u>Synopsis</u>: Bandmates sleep together for the first time. But is their romance a mistake?

After sundown, she becomes ridiculously hip to the blues, revels in their subtle contrast with the night's matte background. Surely the nocturnal sky is not just devoid of color. On a mattress in a studio apartment, they make lovely music together, in tune with their deepest yearnings. The moment exhales. No one is safe. All deities truly understand is desire. His shatterproof soul gathers mist as he realizes life is comprised of tiny concessions. Her mouth gagging on that fact.

Working Title #2: "Apocalypse Survival Guide"

Synopsis: A man roams a world in shambles after a cataclysmic event.

I grow leery of everything. Faint noises. Empty warehouses. Feral cats. Survival. Apprehension is a knapsack that I lug around and keep tossing things into. It's an unwieldy form of insanity that I carry with me, some days heavier than others. Everything can go wrong and inexplicably will, one mishap after another, falling in succession like a row of dominos. Post-catastrophe, I wander through ruins fearing I am the sole survivor. I move reluctantly, alone in a crumbled existence. I carry my bag, unaided, even with an injured spirit.

Working Title #3: "The Mourning Manual"

<u>Synopsis</u>: Male protagonist seeks solitude while trying to make sense of loss.

Midnight finds itself punctuated by flickering neon along the boulevard. Loved ones become ghosts, haunting him with reminders of pointless grudges, cumbersome apologies, whimpered prayers. Nothing resurrects the dead, but the living can always choose to join them. Suicide is not the solution, but neither is drinking himself to the border of foolishness. To survive, he becomes well versed in the art of departure. Just a man in a sweatshirt, hood up against the cold, trudging towards uncertainty.

Working Title #4: "Haunted Moments"

Synopsis: A man encounters paranormal activity after moving into an old manor.

It feels like a hoax, but everything is real: white specters and flickering lamps. Radio feedback and screen doors that swing open on their own. Ask where the spirit goes after death and she says *someplace, eventually*, her voice fading to a note that resonates in the inner ear. But tonight, she's an understudy of darkness, a ghost in the shadows who sounds alive but isn't. Kiss her and she tastes like a broken fever, sickness, night chills. Antifreeze draining on a country road. Doubt inhabits the space between seconds, the shine of headlights as a red pickup casually crosses the centerline. Imagine, if you could, the unsettled dead. A beautiful soul bathing in sorrow with paradise only a retracted transgression away, yet completely out of reach.

Working Title #5: "Vanishing Act"

<u>Synopsis</u>: A missing hooker's secrets spark scandal in a small town.

On the boulevard, a man offers a fistful of dollars and thrusts his fingers down her half-buttoned blouse. Nightfall becomes a tyranny of rumpled bed sheets and unwelcome advances. Temptation is sometimes a locked door, other times a cracked bottle that lets sanity slowly seep away. At the corner bar, men know the inside of her mouth by feel. Recognize the scent of seduction by the approximation of lilacs. She opens up her body for them, one after another in the dark, and then holds resentment inside her mouth like a topic for later discussion. By morning, a suitcase floats along a riverbank, empty except for scuffed stilettos. Police ask the standard questions. Nobody answers. Silence provides a poor substitute for the truth.

Working Title #6: "Confessions of a Dying Flame"

<u>Synopsis</u>: Despite being committed, a couple's relationship grows stale.

In any case, you are always here, tremulous yet turbulent, with full lips dyed the hottest shade of red. I am a seasoned sparring partner who rarely flinches at your insults, more than capable of withstanding a good punch. There is nothing to do with such beautiful emptiness but to wallow inside its void. Our love becomes a fortune cookie we break to find answers we should've already known. With you, I remain tethered to idealistic expectations. How I'd like to believe in the myths of storybook endings, of second-chance romance, of mercy. And I said I do. So I do. Nevertheless.

V

Entries from the Pandemic Diaries

Sunday, February 23, 2020

While civilization contemplates sheltering-in-place, I meet dozens of friendly strangers who I'll never see again. At the gym, hardware store, and neighborhood bar. Head nods and synthetic salutations. Who knows what urges flourish in my mind or between my thighs? A shift in the brain towards an overcast tomorrow. Nobody knows what the body craves in times like these until we realize we can't have it. Knows where our thoughts and attention might wander. Savor the dulcet moments between breaths, between days that we tighten around us like bondage ropes. How we tie ourselves up again and set out into the world, holding everything in that wants to fall out. The sickness that craves tight spaces, seeks bodies adjacent to other bodies. How the deadliness of each inhalation remains nearly imperceptible, yet something we all sense.

Tuesday, February 25, 2020

In February, I routinely drown doubts with the contents of a Mardi Gras drinking glass. Such smugness in the way I buy cocktails for transparent friends, all with a wink and a smile. Such hubris. There, in the predictable groundwork leading to another hangover. Tiny deities float on the surface like ice cubes, melting into nothing. We haven't yet mastered how to sanitize our hands on the hour. How to keep them cautiously in our pockets. It's February, and my fingers know nothing but lust, instinctually touching everything. ATM buttons, bus seats, door handles. Still reaching across tables to shake hands. Who knows what sickness spreads through the unknowing public? In other towns, other nations, populations shrouded by the white sheets of hospital beds. Passengers on cruise ships stranded in harbors. Close to home yet oceans away. What does it mean? Ambiguity? Immunity? I notice the narrowing of space between me and misfortune. It's February, and I spend my freedom like lottery winnings, squandering a down payment on a certain future.

Friday, March 13, 2020

Slowly, then suddenly, we lock down all doors like a prison. Spring flowers flourish while we huddle inside, unable to appreciate nature's rebirth. My favorite season, now a stolen prize. Birds collide with windows over and over but continue to chase their reflections. I put on clothes. I take them off. Each weekday becomes a Monday. Each Monday becomes hell. Another manic form of panic. I wear what I christen as my *apocalypse hoodie* to take out the garbage and grab the mail. I hang it on a nail near the door and then wash my hands obsessively. So often that the water starts to make things dry. My skin, my humor. I put on my apocalypse hoodie, then take it off. Hold my breath as long as possible whenever I venture outside. But inside, I'm defenseless. Mouth agape and prone to infection.

Wednesday, March 25, 2020

Who knows what angst flourishes within the body? Beneath the ribs, the aching cage of bones. At home, I corner myself into discontent. Declutter everything until everything disappears. Reorganize my domestic puzzle. Disinfect surfaces and stare at mirrors. Who knows what fear lurks outside the door? A nudge sends our collective sanity over the edge, flailing. All spring, I wander in and out of rooms that I wreck only to tidy later. Sweep debris under area rugs. This tug inside the mind as anxiety spreads like a brushfire. The frenzied atmosphere as we fracture our daily schedules bit by bit, moment by moment. Until there's nothing left but the pregnant pause that I use to write this paragraph. Nothing left but a knife that slices through wrists and reality.

Saturday, April 11, 2020

The internet tells the truth and we have no choice but to pretend it's fiction. All propaganda and pomade-slick intentions, data distorted by its misleading context. The weather fluctuates like the stock market. Feral animals overrun vacation towns and rest stops, searching for the scraps that tourists would normally leave behind. Before travel restrictions. Before mask mandates. Social media tells us lies and we have no choice but to believe them. Political doubletalk tries to convince us nothing can go wrong. Tries to convince us there's nothing to see here, nothing we'd recognize as a threat until it climbs inside us.

Tuesday, May 12, 2020

Apple trees blossom near the transit station. Their blooms still fall apart in mid-May, scattering beautifully on the asphalt. By now, I've abandoned the myth of spring. Periodically checking the deadbolt and wrapping my vulnerability in fleece blankets. Scan the news and skip breakfast with a nervous stomach. It's a comforting form of uneasiness, one without morning commutes or office gossip. I stuff fear in the back of closets with my winter clothes. Linger too long in the scalding hot shower, wide-eyed, gazing at the ceiling. Who knew chaos could be so cozy? Disaster movies play on a continuous loop in my dreams, zombie attacks and extinction events braiding themselves in my subconscious until I cease sleeping altogether. I'd say I'm not right, but we all know I'm wrong. Cleaning to kill a virus that only exists outside these walls, or inside my mind.

Thursday, May 21, 2020

Lilacs flourish around the perimeter of the city park even if I'm not there to appreciate them. Rooted adjacent to the monkey bars and picnic tables. Emitting a scent that I'd savor if I wasn't in the midst of a sequestered season. Any other spring, I'd be writing love poems to the petulant sky. I'd be sweating off the cabin fever from my skin and glistening below the temperamental sun. Listening to pop music psalms and daydreaming while on impromptu vacations. Any other spring and I'd be outside exploring things other than fear, my hopes as untouched as lettuce in my refrigerator. Fresh and healthy but destined to spoil from neglect.

Thursday, May 28, 2020

Nobody is resisting, yet everything feels like resistance. A police station burns to the ground, becomes a pile of rubble by dawn, a symbol of scorched truth. The marginalized die and keep dying, beneath the knees and nightsticks of the corrupt, beneath the heavy hands of those holding them down. I have nothing to say that doesn't sound black. That doesn't sound anti-establishment and rebellious. The social justice poem I wrote today seems like a remix of one I penned four years ago. I just carbon copy my pain so you can witness it without me sending it to you directly. Some see unrelated incidents while I notice a common thread, frayed. One by one, down they fall. Blood soaks both t-shirts and concrete. People say their names in memoriam, and again after the next tragedy, but never early enough to rescue them.

Saturday, June 6, 2020

Sickness takes to the body like water to a basement. Seeps in deliberately until it's too late to avoid extensive damage. When I was twelve, I wandered off the shore into Lake Michigan and let purgatory flow around me. That familiar drop in the stomach between something we recognize and something we cannot understand. The balance between surface tension and motion sickness. Still, we careen into others' lives inside liquor stores or at gas stations. Our whorish fingertips and their proximity fetish with the unfamiliar. Inventory everything that we touch on any given day, or what may touch us, and we'd produce a catalog of dangers that once seemed benign. Illness quietly collects in our crevices and nooks. The bait conceals the obvious hazard of the hook.

Tuesday, June 16, 2020

During the quarantine, I can't stay calm. Can't keep my shit together while things fall apart. All night long, I flinch at noises in the hallway. Sirens down the street. Figure out that I've prepped for every worst-case scenario except this one. Hurricanes, uprisings, aliens, zombies. Monsters and mobs. Stacks of canned tuna in the pantry and ample ammo in the basement. For every catastrophe, I imagine a hundred endgames, each one grimmer than the previous—but none of which I'm completely ready for. A friend claims that he's stockpiling toilet paper and latex gloves in case things go south. Uses his hazard pay to buy sacks of potatoes and first aid kits. We're all married to the gospel of desperation in a time when every nightmare conjures fever, when people reflexively interrogate each other after every cough. We keep the frantic truth under our tongues, to have and hold, for richer and poorer. Nowadays, and in health.

Wednesday, July 1, 2020

Whatever hatred escalates in our hearts also escalates in the streets. In buildings, broken and overrun with rodents and junkies. Whatever tension escalates in the neighborhood, escalates the crowds. Escalates resentment, amplifies the wounded symphony that we sing as we walk on cracked sidewalks. One month, there are no disinfectant wipes. By the next, they are shipped in bulk and on my doorstep along with a litany of impulse buys. Our common sense unravels all summer, gradually, the loose strings collected beneath us in a pile. Who knows what unrest buds along the boulevards of the battered? Or underneath the pressed kneecap of a rogue policeman? We assume our neighbors have wicked intentions, but they could be pure. Could be innocent. Darkness escalates in the souls of those forgotten by society, those who march one by one on state capitals just for their message to be ignored.

Wednesday, July 15, 2020

Lord knows what falsehoods sprout like noxious weeds in the back of his throat. In his voice box. In his breath. Critics track and measure the depth of his lies. The collective turmoil undoes us in every usual way. By day, I walk the local trails to forget about the pandemonium. Note the crabapples and foxglove, inventory the litter that disposable people leave behind as evidence of their trashy existence. How chaos thrives, even though I'm not thriving within it. A few blocks over, people protest for justice with no results, become emptied of faith. It's the perfect season to simulate optimism. To half-believe the voided promises of politicians as they pander for votes and power. The thing that people shout for always seemingly out of reach.

Friday, August 7, 2020

The allergies we overcame by May come back right before autumn. Our voices lost down the well and our heads stuffed with cotton like teddy bears. All summer we were plagued by bouts of situational vertigo, then nothing. As if we were dropped off into open spaces blindfolded, with no directions or notion of how to return home. Something vast yet utterly unmappable. Echoes accompany me to the mailbox, haunt my shower songs. Tentatively greet strangers in the street when I wasn't expecting to see anybody, my eyes blinking warnings in morse code. We're all falling apart, so might as well savor the downfall. Tiny apocalypses spread like rumors. Our burning is deliberate, but comforting, and of indeterminate origin.

Sunday, August 23, 2020

It's late August and wasps have invaded the siding near the garage. We spray and the pavement becomes littered with husks of insects flat on their backs. We sweep up their corpses, toss them in the trash to hide the evidence of our insect genocide. The scene simulates the current news cycle. So many deaths in full view, only to be brushed away and overlooked. The detritus we leave behind in our wake, a world smushed by our carbon footprint, collapsed like the wasteful boxes yielded by our online orders. Another month left undone and reality begins to crumble. Another year and we'll no longer recall our routines—endless rush hours, mundane errands, and the name of the coworker who never cleans up their spills by the coffeemaker. We remain at home, isolated, yet our spirits haunt the elevators of emptied buildings with silence.

Tuesday, September 22, 2020

What can bloom when the soil of the mind has been poisoned? In my journal, I write that question on a blank page after weeks of writer's block, unsure whether it's literature or gibberish. Raw and vulnerable from witnessing the carnage. The air around us does nothing but get inhaled. It becomes a conduit, channeling toxicity into our bloodstreams. Nothing to do with health, but everything with sickness. Each microbe lurking in public places suddenly within us in a flash. Who knew what dangers loitered nearby, waiting, casing the unsuspecting houses of our bodies just to burglarize our wellbeing? Ready to rob us of the misplaced grins that we used to hide beneath our masks. The reporters inform us of a variant brewing in some foreign location. We sigh, knowing contamination will eventually find its way, make its inevitable odyssey to our bodies. We'll be a destination it's never visited, yet somehow it will know its way around with intimate familiarity.

VI

Identity Theories

1.

My theoretical identity begins with happy hour and ends with hangover hymns. It's all three-day benders, flayed moments, and dodged responsibilities. A back parking lot overrun with weeds. A rusted sedan that idles until a cop knocks against the window, asking if everything's all right. Well, it's not, despite a solemn nod otherwise. But thanks for checking. He stays red-eyed, keyed up, crooning tavern lullabies off-key on dingy dance floors as fate arrives. Every lie echoes some other lie uttered previously while the riot in his throat chants for another shot glass soliloquy. My theoretical identity is nothing if not disjointed. Nothing if not out of sync. He's always *going for one* that inevitably becomes *just one more*. Gin and juice with throwback songs on a jukebox clog the catch basin of common sense. All his enablers are lip-glossed and looking for trouble. The end of it all can be found at the end of a long rope. The end of it all can be tied into an invisible noose that tightens around his neck, squeezing out excuses until he's left hanging, constricted by the pressure of the truth.

2.

My theoretical identity needs less negative self-talk. Craves less ambiguity around certain things. Requires less chatter from relatives and friends who only appear as phantoms haunting social media feeds. To say life is a party would be a lie, but truthfully it feels like a dinner gathering of its finest assassins. Knives in backs, people covertly stabbing each other with stigmas. My theoretical identity wears psychological camouflage to conceal feelings, makes a ritual out of silence until unspoken words corrode inside his mouth. Marvels at how the world shifts like a puzzle inside its box every time people let their guard down. Sharpens half-hearted apologies into spikes that puncture skin if clutched too closely. Everyone keeps regurgitating questionable advice as if clichés possess healing powers. My theoretical identity hides clenched fists inside his pockets while flashing a synthetic smile and politely changing the subject, again.

3.

People adore my theoretical identity like he's the best friend they've never had. Ever the perfect wingman, he blindly supports each shitty life choice they make. His nights are full of people-pleasing and silent affirmations, curating the mistakes of his closest colleagues. Raising hell as if it's his firstborn child and then tidying up messes afterward. My theoretical identity possesses my father's temper, so occasionally he obsesses over details, bumps against door jambs, and makes a teakettle sound when anger boils over. Sleight of hand over hand, simple minds over matter. The therapist in the strip mall charges too much, spends too much time overanalyzing and not enough listening. Okay, let's unpack this. When my theoretical identity ultimately loses it, people's eyes turn wide like scared deer. They feign astonishment, pretend to be shocked by the emotional arson. Everyone whistles away their guilt while hiding gas cans and Zippos behind their backs.

4.

My theoretical identity always mentions *hope* as if it's real, deliberately and with a scintilla of optimism. Like it's not some convoluted concept crafted from rainbows and idealistic dreams. Fashioned from vellum paper, thin and easy to tear. By now all his interior voices have triggered outside actions. All his outside actions now held against him like a pistol pressed to his temple. He fears falling apart mostly because he fears he'll never get put back together. He fears getting put back together because it feels like falling apart, over and over again. My theoretical identity loves the redemption arc. The badass-turned-good-guy recycled narrative. Loves others' insides for what's actually inside them, not the make-believe, made-for-TV version. My theoretical identity always mentions *hope* like he's tethered to it, naïve enough to remain enslaved by the world's most convincing lie.

5.

My theoretical identity code switches during staff meetings and conference calls. Wears a sensible sport coat and faux grin. Waltzes around company protocol while doing a tokenized two-step. He tiptoes through the pitfalls of corporate culture, noticing broken clocks but pretending they display the proper time. He was complaining in a manner HR would find cringeworthy when he claimed that he'd never get promoted, yet he kept reluctantly laughing at his supervisor's jokes until his wires got permanently crossed. My theoretical identity calls this charade professional development. SMART goals from another biased performance review. Being miscategorized as the angry black guy in the office leaves him like the break room coffee pot after noon—emptied, with no one eager to refill him. He's been stockpiling supplies and postponed dreams in his cubicle. My theoretical identity knows if you sell out, you can never buy yourself back. All he needs is one more reason to say no, to vamoose, to eighty-six this sideshow in the name of diversity.

6.

My theoretical identity finds comfort in the misery of others. He never anchors his tongue or meters his candor, says incendiary words doused with accelerant. Recognize the pulled pins of his comments as live grenades. In the abandoned warehouse, all the machines are chained to the floor and he has the strangest form of fevered sleep, like hundreds of nightmares haunting his psyche. Don't feed the monster. Don't feed the panic. The rusted shovel of his voice keeps digging for answers. He knows honesty can be its own form of punishment. He knows doubt can be the murderer of all dreams, secretly smothering them in their bassinet while still in their infancy. It is the worst sort of origin story, but the best sort of snuff film. My theoretical identity is a one-man renaissance blooming in these new-age dark ages. My theoretical identity loves asking questions when solutions don't exist.

7.

My theoretical identity seems paranoid, but only because he recognizes the subtle difference between caution and fear. Mostly, he remains troubled by shaky bridges and faulty ball bearings. Obsessed with inconsistent narratives and broken-down machinery. He keeps losing track of what he should be nervous about today while sifting through propaganda on the internet or viewing the nightly news. His nervousness is a ghost moving between rooms and knocking knick-knacks off the tables. My theoretical identity preaches the gospel of insurance policies and backup plans as if they matter anymore, but really he's saying *please help* with his eyes. With his suspicious mind. He's a little amazed when he wanders into hell. And even more amazed when he walks out without a scratch.

8.

When my theoretical identity was born, he wore a hoodie and walked through a gated community. All reviled and racially profiled. He carried a bag of Skittles and a cell phone in his pocket, but his unarmed presence still aroused suspicion. My theoretical identity was just starting to notice the hazards of existence when a neighborhood watchman gripped a pistol and gave chase. Claimed he fit a description, presumed guilt in the wake of innocence. Here is the suspect. Here is the gun. Amongst the townhomes, he visited relatives while black, a crime punishable by death, evidently. The system sketched a perfect circle in the street and stood its ground. Went all confrontation and confusion after a gun goes off. Here is the villain. Here is the victim. There goes another, slain by the familiar sham of self-defense, Second Amendment rights, and stereotypes. By doing nothing, my theoretical identity starts everything. Again and again, death is hardcoded to repeat like an infinite loop in society's flawed algorithm. The world waits uneasily for the next news story, hashtag, protest, and acquittal. My theoretical identity already knows the endless cycle. Already knows black folks like him can lose their life for no good reason. Already knows black folks like him can lose.

9.

All in all, my theoretical identity wants more controversy, since controversy sells. More amorous intentions and regrettable dates. He arranges disorder in a tight circle. Plagiarizes urban folklore but fails to verify any facts. All press is good press, he guesses. My theoretical identity gets torn down by the infrastructure of gossip, then rebuilt into a legend. Like all mythology, his life story confronts the queasy and uneasy until it drowns in the undercurrent of reality. Oscillates between chaos and clarity. He wears a façade, but it's a façade over another façade tucked behind a veneer of open-ended questions. An outline of a face over the faces he has shown before. My theoretical identity lost his common sense, but for what he lacks in judgment, he makes up for with his go-forth-and-fucking-do-it-all spirit. Call it character. Call it charisma. My theoretical identity daydreams about death as much as he lives his life. Like a B-list celebrity, he'll be half gone before you even know he's here.

10.

My theoretical identity scatters beer bottles and complaints across the front porch. Becomes all catastrophe and conspiracy theories when the power goes out. His credit is all jacked up, with past-due bills stacked atop the kitchen counter. He drowned in debt from the beginning, but for what he lacks in money, he makes up with slick vernacular. My theoretical identity puts his hand out to acquaintances like a panhandler, his lies as warm and soft as butter in the dish. By the time you read this, you'll probably sniff out his intentions. My theoretical identity is nothing if not cunning. Though he knows how to survive without sacrificing his dreams, he still gets caught in the thick of thin things. Ever the imperfect messenger, his confidence game becomes a tightrope walker—one misstep and balance becomes urgent and irrelevant all at once. He is nothing if not ready.

11.

Sometimes he goes off-grid, offhanded. Specializes in adaptation, manipulation. My theoretical identity fights like a sonofabitch, but it's the truce you need to watch out for, lined with intimidation and doubletalk. He takes only what he needs. A tawny-paged journal with a fake leather cover. A toothbrush. A skeleton key. He can hide so many things in his mouth by now, it's ridiculous: apologies, pain killers, batteries, the truth. He takes only what he needs but eventually he needs everything. Razor blades, cheap beer, pocket-knives. My theoretical identity monitors the eyes of the clerk while he shoplifts redemption from a bodega. He has bruises on his arms from some back alley, backyard, or back of the barroom violence. Everywhere he goes, he keeps collecting sins. Keeps them quartered and folded like stolen maps stashed in his backpack.

12.

Fear puts my theoretical identity inside the trunk, then takes him out. Covers his eyes, then smothers him with chloroform. If he irritates it, fear might kill him with indifference. Like he's a carnival goldfish from a water-filled baggie. Or a pet store hamster in a filthy cage. Neglected to the point of numbness. Loved to the point of death. At the bus stop, my theoretical identity waited for a ride that never showed. Now, as fear's hostage, his joints ache with panic, his tongue rusts with disuse. How he refuses the candies offered as loyalty bribes, leaves them to melt in their wrappers. Crawls into a closet for the night and never crawls out. His fingers fumbling over the deadbolts inside his mind.

13.

My theoretical identity is a strip club next to a rundown hotel, a disaster foreshadowing another disaster. A sign blinking its neon indifference—open all night, open all night. He waits on the chaise lounge by a dusty pool table, flirting with counterfeit sweethearts, confusing carnal things with comfort and sullying his reputation. He gets snared in the honeytrap trying to snatch the bait, but it's all symptoms of a hollowness that he aches to fill, his origami soul that's been folded until it looks like something else altogether. Up-down, up-down, listening intently for a moan that sounds more like love than longing. My theoretical identity becomes a window overlooking the allure of the wrong side of town. His eyes blink their neon indifference—open all night, open all night.

14.

It's so American of my theoretical identity to blame his parents for his shortcomings. To blame his teeth for their decay. He empties his mouth like a toy box. Everything there, and then nothing. Drained of substance and nostalgia. It's so passive-aggressive of him to make a game of it. So Midwestern. My theoretical identity inherited these tendencies as a tweenager, along with an obscene fascination with equations and the paranormal. He says luck is always heading towards him, or worse, running away. Inside the house, he lays out his mementos. Tosses action figures into the fireplace like a budding pyromaniac. Oversleeps and cuts his forearms daily. There's a photo on the mantle of my theoretical identity sitting in the center of a backyard birthday party, with a silly hat perched atop his head and a middle school scowl on his face. Tension ready to be sliced and served like buttercream cake.

15.

Before long, my theoretical identity is brazen enough to build a shadow kingdom out of dubious promises and cynical banter. He's still charming. Still playing straight man to the world's degrading comedy routine. Still burning evidence, questioning everything, and flipping coins to make critical life decisions. My theoretical identity is figuring out if wearing the crown is worth the criticism, trying to resist the malcontent recipe that's been baked into his soul. He remembers the astonishment of the county fair psychic who examined his palms and backed away. In the corner bar, my theoretical identity paces by the jukebox until it's time to head home. Masters parlor tricks, shaking table legs at appropriate moments and throwing his voice. Melancholy grows and swells within him until he falls apart. Sometimes my theoretical identity does drunken singalongs with the closing time crowd like "Sweet Caroline," with lyrics so familiar they feel foreign. Sometimes the words *so good* lodge themselves like hard candy in his throat.

16.

My theoretical identity starts as another sleepless night, with insomniac gears turning and an approximation of anxiety. My theoretical identity remains awake and inconsolable when folks tell him to relax. He stands atop an overpass to dial loved ones in a frenzy at 8 am. Claim there's too much rush in rush hour, too much traffic congesting his mind. Everyone tries convincing him what doesn't destroy him makes him smarter, but he keeps adjusting the wax wings on his back and attempting hazardous approach angles towards the sun. There are too many vehicles on these roads, all potholed and petulant and a waste of tax dollars. Too many crowded spaces and combustibles. His mental engine cruds up with manic thoughts. Imagine my theoretical identity attempting repair, with an oil smear across his forehead and loose screws in his pocket. Envision him holding a match, ready to set things afire and slow-motion stroll away, with a delayed explosion in the background like a cheesy action flick. Don't look back. Never look back.

Suggestions for Writing Poetry

Journals with ochre-tinged pages can be indispensable. When considering topics, beware of the long-winded and trite. You never know when vices might provide inspiration, particularly while dancing with narrow-waisted strangers at dive bars.

Remember, ambiguity creates interest. Liquor may also help. A camisole beneath a silk blouse might mend the awkward interstices between lines.

Imagery always makes an impression. Kudzu adorning telephone poles like stockings. Rain-slicked streets glazed with the vulgar neon light of strip club signs. Resentment smoldering like a lit cigarette tossed onto the sidewalk.

Expect nothing. Prepare for everything.

For every trap door or tattered roadmap, draw a red X across your forehead. Do not censor questionable thoughts or preach the false gospel of hopefulness.

On Saturdays, teach the skyline how to be an escape route and flirt with the uncertain havoc of a disjointed future. Mention crimes and failures without context and let the reader sort through the carnage.

Resist having tidy conclusions.

Acknowledgments

Writing a book like this is more challenging than I envisioned and more rewarding than I could imagine. Thank you to Laura and Bella Potter, who put up with my crap during a pandemic so I could develop this project and find my voice.

Thanks to Victoria Mendoza, who probably read this book over and over until her eyes were dripping, and also to Tommy Sheffield, Linda Hall, and the rest of the Stillhouse Press staff who recognized, validated, and supported my creative vision. I appreciate you.

And I want to thank anybody who ever said anything positive to me or taught me something. I listened to it all, and it meant something, even if I pretended like it didn't.

www.ingramcontent.com/pod-product-compliance
Lightning Source LLC
Chambersburg PA
CBHW050327120526
44592CB00014B/2081